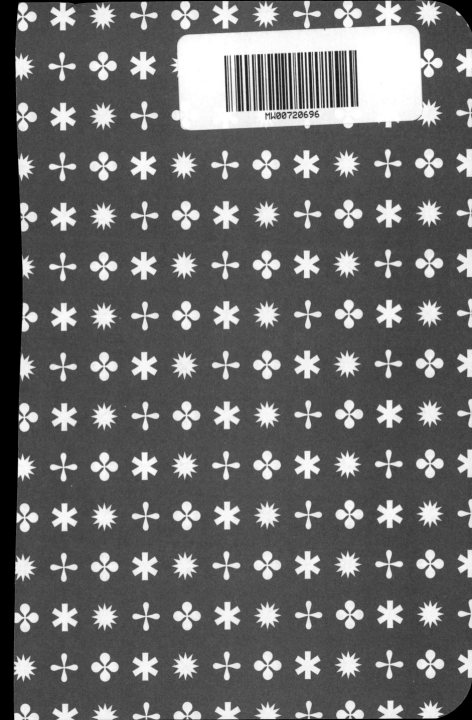

MW00720696

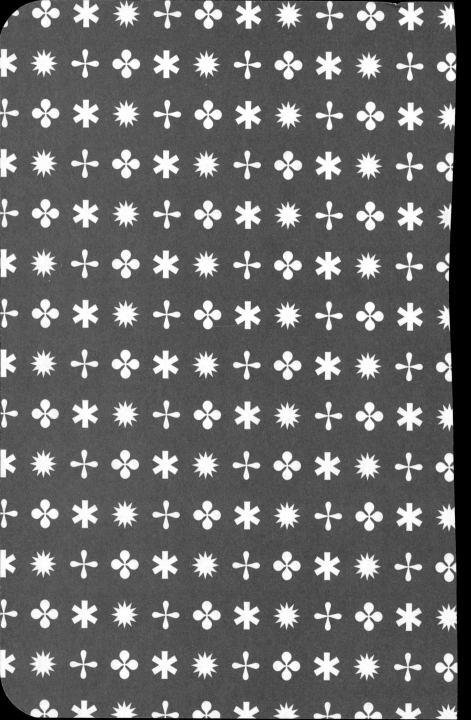

BOOK CRUSH

Journal

For Isabella —

BOOK CRUSH

Journal

Nancy pearl

NANCY PEARL

with Kerry Colburn

SASQUATCH BOOKS
SEATTLE

Printed in the United States of America
Published by Sasquatch Books
Distributed by PGW/Perseus
15 14 13 12 11 10 09 08 07   9 8 7 6 5 4 3 2 1

Design and illustration: Gretchen Scoble Design
ISBN-13: 978-1-57061-541-2
ISBN-10: 1-57061-541-1

Sasquatch Books
119 South Main Street, Suite 400
Seattle, WA 98104
(206) 467-4300
www.sasquatchbooks.com
custserv@sasquatchbooks.com

Introduction

I love to read, and I suspect you may, too. What better way is there to travel to distant places, or to a time far in the past or future, without leaving your house; to meet all different sorts of people; and to try out new ideas and ways of looking at the world?

And the best part about reading is that it is entirely personal. There are no right or wrong reactions to what you're reading—this isn't a school assignment. Your reaction to a book (loving it, hating it, beginning but putting it down never to pick it up again) is all about you—your feelings, your ideas, your beliefs. It may come as a surprise (or not!) to discover that your best friend has a totally different feeling about the book you've both read.

So here's your chance to keep track of what you're reading, what you've read, and what you want to read. It's a place to record whether a book made you laugh or cry, whether you were bored or enchanted by it, whether or not a book changed your life—and lots more, too.

I'd very much like to hear from you about the books you've developed crushes on. My email address is nancy@nancypearl.com.

nancy pearl

Reading List

BEFORE AND AFTER HARRY (Potter, of course)

The Field Guide by Holly Black and Tony DiTerlizzi

Artemis Fowl (and sequels) by Eoin Colfer

The City of Ember (and sequels) by Jeanne DuPrau

Half Magic by Edward Eager

Thorn Ogres of Hagwood (and sequels) by Robin Jarvis

A Wizard of Earthsea by Ursula K. Le Guin

Magyk by Angie Sage

The Amulet of Samarkand (and sequels) by Jonathan Stroud

OTHER TIMES, OTHER PLACES, OTHER PEOPLE

Catherine, Called Birdy by Karen Cushman

Blue Willow by Doris Gates

Stowaway by Karen Hesse

A Proud Taste for Scarlet and Miniver by E. L. Konigsburg

A Single Shard by Linda Sue Park

Anahita's Woven Riddle by Meghan Nuttall Sayres

At the Sign of the Star by Katherine Sturtevant

GIRL POWER!

The True Confessions of Charlotte Doyle by Avi

The Misadventures of Maude March by Audrey Couloumbis

So You Want to Be a Wizard by Diane Duane

Harriet the Spy by Louise Fitzhugh

Julie of the Wolves by Jean Craighead George

Princess Academy by Shannon Hale

Zeely by Virginia Hamilton

The Star of Kazan by Eva Ibbotson

Fairest by Gail Carson Levine

So B. It by Sarah Weeks

All About Me

The last book I read was...

TITLE: Possibility of fireflies.

AUTHOR: ....

DATE FINISHED: Dec. 28 2009

WHAT IT'S ABOUT: This book is about a girl with an abusive mom who tells her kids their dad left because he didn't want them, leaving them with nowhere to go. The main girl falls in love with a 21 years old in search of love. She learns that what she thought was real wasn't. Her sister also ends up breaking laws and running away.

THE BEST PART: For me the best part was when her sister gets in trouble for burning down an old mill and the sister of that girl sticks by her side through everything, I thought that was really teaching.

RATING: I give it: ☆☆★☆☆

The book I'm reading right now is...

TITLE: The Adoration of Jenna Fox

AUTHOR: Mary E. Pearson

DATE STARTED: Dec. 28 2009

WHAT IT'S ABOUT: It's about a girl named Jenna Fox who has been in a coma for a year because of a car accident and wakes up not feeling like herself. She feels as if she's not Jenna Fox but just has her body. She tries to re-create her life and figure out what really happened.

THE BEST PART: When Evan (the boy she loved) accepted her even though she was different and was basiclly made from science with her prothstetics body and only 10% of the real her. The "butterfly" of her brain. She ended up living for 260 years and spending a good 70 with him. I thought it was cute because they still loved eachother no matter what.

RATING: I give it: ☆ ☆ ☆ ★ ☆

The next books I can't wait to read are...

TITLE: Schwa was Here

AUTHOR: Neal Shusterman

WHAT IT'S ABOUT: The mystery of a boy named Schwa who is sometimes seen and sometimes appeared to be invisible. There's rumors but no one really knows who or what he is and - and - is never noticed. His shoes blend into the ground eyes change to the color of the ceiling and if you stare long enough you see the wall behind him.

HOW I HEARD ABOUT IT: Picked it out at random from the library.

Talent? ° o

TITLE: Harry Potter Series

AUTHOR: J. K. Rowling

WHAT IT'S ABOUT:

A boy named Harry Potter who fights evils in the wizarding world to regain peace and defeat the all-powerful Lord Voldemort.

HOW I HEARD ABOUT IT: Very popular with everyone. Became a movie series. The movie series ended after about 8-10 long years and to continue that journey for me, I would like to read and discover more of the plot and events that the characters describe through emotional range throughout the books. I would also like to discover where this craze first originated.

The next books I can't wait to read are...

TITLE: ....

AUTHOR: ....

WHAT IT'S ABOUT: ....

....

....

....

....

....

....

....

....

....

HOW I HEARD ABOUT IT: ....

....

....

....

....

....

....

....

....

TITLE: ....

AUTHOR: ....

WHAT IT'S ABOUT: ....

....

....

....

....

....

....

....

....

....

HOW I HEARD ABOUT IT: ....

....

....

....

....

....

....

....

Other books on my must-read radar:

TITLE: The Off-Season

AUTHOR:

WHAT IT'S ABOUT: A girl who plays mostly guy sports with some family problems and tries to find her true self and stand up for what she believes.
     Also about one of her first loves to a guy named Brian who plays for the opposite team who can't be seen together.

HOW I HEARD ABOUT IT:
     It's a sequal to the book I read a while back called Dairy Queen.
     My friend May H. read this book for an english project and said it was good so I also decided to read it. :)

TITLE: ....

AUTHOR: ....

WHAT IT'S ABOUT: ....

....

....

....

....

....

....

....

....

....

HOW I HEARD ABOUT IT: ....

....

....

....

....

....

....

....

....

Other books on my must-read radar:

TITLE: ....

AUTHOR: ....

WHAT IT'S ABOUT: ....

....

....

....

....

....

....

....

....

....

HOW I HEARD ABOUT IT: ....

....

....

....

....

....

....

....

TITLE: ....

AUTHOR: ....

WHAT IT'S ABOUT: ....

....

....

....

....

....

....

....

....

....

HOW I HEARD ABOUT IT: ....

....

....

....

....

....

....

....

....

Other books on my must-read radar:

TITLE: ....

AUTHOR: ....

WHAT IT'S ABOUT: ....
....
....
....
....
....
....
....
....

HOW I HEARD ABOUT IT: ....
....
....
....
....
....
....
....

TITLE: ....

AUTHOR: ....

WHAT IT'S ABOUT: ....

....

....

....

....

....

....

....

....

....

HOW I HEARD ABOUT IT: ....

....

....

....

....

....

....

....

....

My all-time favorite book is...

TITLE: The Hunger Games

AUTHOR:

WHY IT'S MY FAVORITE: It's a love-action story.

FOR ME, THE MOST MEMORABLE SCENE WAS: When Peeta was injured and his love in the story did everything in her power to help save him. This really showed how much they loved eachother :\

DEFINITELY THE MOST INTERESTING CHARACTER WAS: Peeta, he gave the poor girl food and hope when she was just about to be able to live on the streets. They end up meeting again 10 years later in the games with a possible fight to the death.

THE BIGGEST SURPRISE IN THE BOOK WAS: The biggest surprise was when they were fighting off their attackers a little girl was put into the arena and had to kill people too even though she was so young. She was tough but not tough enough.

IF MY FAVORITE BOOK HAD A SEQUEL, THE TITLE SHOULD BE: ......

It does; catching fire

HERE'S WHAT WOULD HAPPEN IF I WAS WRITING IT: ....

I liked the way it was written and I don't think that I would change a single thing about it. It had just enough surprises and detail to make the book AMAZING!! :)

Other books I really, really like:

TITLE: Prism

AUTHOR:

WHY I LIKE IT SO MUCH: I liked this book because it was about two different worlds. One with medicine and one without it. It really gave me insight on what life would be like with no medication and still these awfull diseases. Would people on the street just sit there waiting for their deaths? I guess we're pretty lucky. There was also a love in the story, A girl entered the world without medicine and fell in love. It was pure love. And it didn't have a fairytale ending which I liked because it proves and shows that nothing's perfect. It made it interesting

CHECK ALL THAT APPLY:
- ☑ It made me laugh
- ☑ It made me cry
- ☑ It made me think
- ☑ It surprised me
- ☑ I could not put it down

TITLE: The Tear Collecter

AUTHOR:

WHY I LIKE IT SO MUCH: Because it was about a girl who survived off of tears and would break up with boys or get back with them just for tears. but surprisingly she finds a guy she actually loves and is fed-up with her family and collecting tears so she decides to give up on what her family wants so she could have love.
     It shows how powerfull love is and gives me hope because right now all people want is sex etc. So I think these kinds of books are great!

CHECK ALL THAT APPLY:

○ It made me laugh   ○ It made me cry   ☑ It made me think
☑ It surprised me   ☑ I could not put it down

Other books I really, really like:

TITLE: Just Listen

AUTHOR: Sarah Dessen

WHY I LIKE IT SO MUCH:

Because it was a tale about a girl with alotta issues and finding a guy who really cares about her. They also end up sharing an interest in music and I thought that this book was super cute and some parts were just hilarious! :) The guy she likes had anger issues before so his friend bought him 2 rings. 1 saying "go fuck yourself" and the other saying "or not" which shows his progress with anger.

CHECK ALL THAT APPLY:

- ⦿ It made me laugh
- ○ It made me cry
- ○ It made me think
- ○ It surprised me
- ☑ I could not put it down

TITLE: Crank & Glass

AUTHOR: ....

WHY I LIKE IT SO MUCH: It's a story about a girl who does drugs when she goes off to live with her dad and it turns out that her dad is also a drug addict. So they end up doing drugs together. It made me realize how lucky I am that my parents care about me and also care about themselves. I could be a bad kid but because of them I'm not.

It was written in poem form which made it a quick read and I really liked that :)

CHECK ALL THAT APPLY:

- ☑ It made me laugh
- ☑ It surprised me
- ○ It made me cry
- ☑ I could not put it down
- ☑ It made me think

Other books I really, really like:

TITLE: 13 reasons why

AUTHOR: ....

WHY I LIKE IT SO MUCH: It was about a girl who made 13 tapes for 13 people and on each tape to each person it explained why the girl who gave out the tapes had killed herself.

I loved this book because I've always thought about what life would be like if I was gone or killed myself just over little things. In a way this book explained to me the real troubles in life and really that the girl in the book shouldn't have killed herself and that there were people there for her ☺

CHECK ALL THAT APPLY:

○ It made me laugh ✓ It made me cry ✓ It made me think
✓ It surprised me ✓ I could not put it down

TITLE: Unwind

AUTHOR:

WHY I LIKE IT SO MUCH: It was something that i've really never read about. It was about a world where it was normal for parents if a child did something bad to unwind them. This means you take apart the kid piece by piece and donate his/her organs and body parts to other people. 3 kids had this fate and decided not to accept it. They tried to hide and run away from it. In the end love was shared and they found a way to stop this violence. They bombed the unwinding room. It had so many surprises, I ♡ed it! :)

CHECK ALL THAT APPLY:

- ✓ It made me laugh
- ✓ It made me cry
- ✓ It made me think
- ✓ It surprised me
- ✓ I could not put it down

Other books I really, really like:

TITLE: ....

AUTHOR: ....

WHY I LIKE IT SO MUCH: ....

....

....

....

....

....

....

....

....

....

....

....

....

....

....

....

....

CHECK ALL THAT APPLY:

○ It made me laugh   ○ It made me cry   ○ It made me think

○ It surprised me   ○ I could not put it down

TITLE: It's kind of a funny Story

AUTHOR: Ned Vizzini

WHY I LIKE IT SO MUCH: It was about a boy who was depressed and wanted to kill himself. He then went to a mental institute. It talks about the problems he had at school, friends, drugs, sex, and family. I could really relate because we were about the same age and I too, also have feelings like this and had issues. I could litterally not put this book down. It was intense + funny. At the end of the book it said that the author wrote it when he was in a mental hospital for 5 days

CHECK ALL THAT APPLY:
- ☑ It made me laugh
- ○ It made me cry
- ☑ It made me think
- ☑ It surprised me
- ☑ I could not put it down

making everything in his book a biography

Here's how I would describe the kinds of books
I like best:

CHECK ALL THAT APPLY!

☑ funny   ☑ sad   ☑ downright scary   ○ long

☑ mysterious   ○ short   ○ nonfiction

☑ fiction   ○ set in another time

○ set in a far-flung location

○ set in a place that reminds me of home

○ set in present day   ○ include animals

○ include a long journey

☑ focus on families   ○ include imaginary creatures

☑ have a love story   ○ have girls as main characters

○ have boys as main characters

☑ have characters that remind me of me and my friends

☑ focus on friendship   ○ have a happy ending

☑ All of the above, depending on my mood!

People I've Met

I've met tons of fascinating characters in books. Here's who I'd vote...

MOST INTERESTING CHARACTER: ....

....

NAME: ....

BOOK: ....

WHY: ....

....

....

....

....

....

....

....

....

....

....

....

....

....

MOST DASTARDLY CHARACTER: ....
....

NAME: ....

BOOK: ....

WHY: ....
....
....
....
....
....
....
....
....
....
....
....
....
....
....
....
....
....

I've met tons of fascinating characters in books.
Here's who I'd vote...

BRAVEST CHARACTER: ....

....

NAME: ....

BOOK: ....

WHY: ....

....

....

....

....

....

....

....

....

....

....

....

....

....

....

....

....

FUNNIEST CHARACTER: ....

....

NAME: ....

BOOK: ....

WHY: ....

....

....

....

....

....

....

....

....

....

....

....

....

....

....

....

....

....

I've met tons of fascinating characters in books. Here's who I'd vote...

CREEPIEST CHARACTER: ....

....

NAME: ....

BOOK: ....

WHY: ....

....

....

....

....

....

....

....

....

....

....

....

....

....

....

....

....

CUTEST CHARACTER: ....

....

NAME: ....

BOOK: ....

WHY: ....

....

....

....

....

....

....

....

....

....

....

....

....

....

....

....

....

....

I've met tons of fascinating characters in books. Here's who I'd vote...

CHARACTER MOST LIKE ME: ....
....

NAME: ....

BOOK: ....

WHY: ....
....
....
....
....
....
....
....
....
....
....
....
....
....
....
....
....

CHARACTER LEAST LIKE ME: ....
....

NAME: ....
BOOK: ....
WHY: ....
....
....
....
....
....
....
....
....
....
....
....
....
....
....
....

I've met tons of fascinating characters in books. Here's who I'd vote...

MOST ADMIRABLE CHARACTER: ....
....
NAME: ....
BOOK: ....
WHY: ....
....
....
....
....
....
....
....
....
....
....
....

CHARACTER I'D MOST LIKE TO TRADE PLACES WITH FOR ONE DAY:

....

NAME: ....

BOOK: ....

WHY: ....

....

....

....

....

....

CHARACTER I'D LEAST LIKE TO TRADE PLACES WITH FOR ONE DAY:

....

NAME: ....

BOOK: ....

WHY: ....

....

....

....

....

....

I've met tons of fascinating characters in books. Here's who I'd vote...

CHARACTER I'D MOST LIKE TO HAVE OVER FOR A PARTY: ....
....

NAME: ....

BOOK: ....

WHY: ....
....
....
....
....
....

CHARACTER I'D LEAST LIKE TO HAVE OVER FOR A PARTY: ....
....

NAME: ....

BOOK: ....

WHY: ....
....
....
....
....
....

CHARACTER I'D MOST LIKE TO KISS: ....

....

NAME: ....

BOOK: ....

WHY: ....

....

....

....

....

....

CHARACTER I'D LEAST LIKE TO KISS: ....

....

NAME: ....

BOOK: ....

WHY: ....

....

....

....

....

....

Characters that totally remind me of my friends:

FRIEND'S NAME: ....

CHARACTER'S NAME: ....

BOOK TITLE: ....

FRIEND'S NAME: ....

CHARACTER'S NAME: ....

BOOK TITLE: ....

FRIEND'S NAME: ....

CHARACTER'S NAME: ....

BOOK TITLE: ....

FRIEND'S NAME: ....

CHARACTER'S NAME: ....

BOOK TITLE: ....

FRIEND'S NAME: ....

CHARACTER'S NAME: ....

BOOK TITLE: ....

FRIEND'S NAME: ....

CHARACTER'S NAME: ....

BOOK TITLE: ....

FRIEND'S NAME: ....

CHARACTER'S NAME: ....

BOOK TITLE: ....

FRIEND'S NAME: ....

CHARACTER'S NAME: ....

BOOK TITLE: ....

FRIEND'S NAME: ....

CHARACTER'S NAME: ....

BOOK TITLE: ....

FRIEND'S NAME: ....

CHARACTER'S NAME: ....

BOOK TITLE: ....

Characters that remind me of people in my family:

NAME: ....

CHARACTER'S NAME: ....

BOOK TITLE: ....

NAME: ....

CHARACTER'S NAME: ....

BOOK TITLE: ....

NAME: ....

CHARACTER'S NAME: ....

BOOK TITLE: ....

NAME: ....

CHARACTER'S NAME: ....

BOOK TITLE: ....

NAME: ....

CHARACTER'S NAME: ....

BOOK TITLE: ....

NAME: ....

CHARACTER'S NAME: ....

BOOK TITLE: ....

NAME: ....

CHARACTER'S NAME: ....

BOOK TITLE: ....

NAME: ....

CHARACTER'S NAME: ....

BOOK TITLE: ....

NAME: ....

CHARACTER'S NAME: ....

BOOK TITLE: ....

NAME: ....

CHARACTER'S NAME: ....

BOOK TITLE: ....

If I had to pick one absolute favorite character from any book, it would be...

NAME: ....

BOOK: ....

WHY: ....

....

....

....

....

....

....

IF WE HAD THE CHANCE TO MEET, I'D BE DYING TO ASK: ....

....

....

....

....

....

....

....

....

....

....

....

....

Places I've Been

I've traveled to all kinds of cool places by reading books. Here's my vote for...

MOST EXOTIC PLACE: ...Australia...

NAME: ......

BOOK: ...Stolen

WHY: ...A girl is stolen from the airport by a boy who has watched and admired her for many years. She's kept in the middle of "nowhere" completely parallel in contrast to her life at home filled with expensive clothes and luxury items. In Australia, the place where she's confined, she tries to escape but realizes that the harsh heat against her pale skin is too much for her. She's left dehydrated and with sun rashes. Throughout her journey she becomes more connected with nature and it's living inhabitants. The exotic place changed her and her beliefs on worldly issues and views of necessities.

WEIRDEST PLACE: ....

....

NAME: ....

BOOK: ....

WHY: ....

....

....

....

....

....

....

....

....

....

....

....

....

....

....

....

....

I've traveled to all kinds of cool places by reading books. Here's my vote for...

MOST MAGICAL PLACE: ....

....

NAME: ....

BOOK: ....

WHY: ....

....

....

....

....

....

....

....

....

....

....

....

....

....

....

....

PLACE I'D MOST LIKE TO VISIT FOR ONE DAY: ....

....

NAME: ....

BOOK: ....

WHY: ....

....

....

....

....

....

....

....

....

....

....

....

....

....

....

....

....

I've traveled to all kinds of cool places by reading books. Here's my vote for...

PLACE I'D LEAST LIKE TO VISIT—EVER: ....
....

NAME: ....
BOOK: ....
WHY: ....
....
....
....
....
....
....
....
....
....
....
....
....
....
....
....

PLACE I'D MOST LIKE TO LIVE: ....

....

NAME: ....

BOOK: ....

WHY: ....

....

....

....

....

....

....

....

....

....

....

....

....

....

....

....

....

....

I've traveled to all kinds of cool places by reading books. Here's my vote for...

PLACE I'D LEAST LIKE TO LIVE: ....
....

NAME: ....

BOOK: ....

WHY: ....
....
....
....
....
....
....
....
....
....
....
....
....
....
....
....

My Story

If I were to write a book about my life, I'd use one of these awesome titles:

1. ....

2. ....

3. ....

....

I'D DEDICATE IT TO: ....

....

....

MY PEN NAME WOULD BE: ....

....

....

THE BRILLIANT OPENING LINE WOULD BE: ....

....

....

....

....

....

Here are the friends, family members, pets, and celebrities who might make appearances in the book:

1. Cynthia Peterson
2. Brandon Keirlin
3.
4.
5.
6.
7.
8.
9.
10.
11.
12.
13.
14.
15.
16.

Here's what my very own book cover would look like:

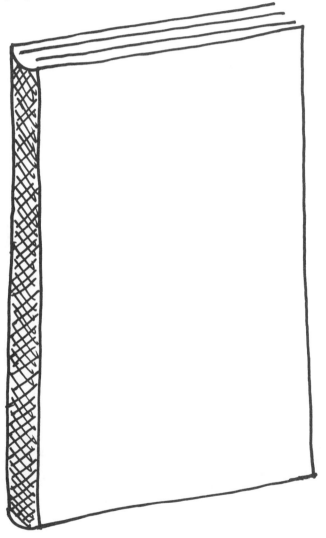

Naturally, it would be made into a movie starring:

1. .... (as me!)
2. ....
3. ....
4. ....
5. ....
6. ....
7. ....
8. ....
9. ....
10. ....
11. ....
12. ....
13. ....
14. ....
15. ....
16. ....
17. ....
18. ....
19. ....
20. ....

If I were going to write another kind of book, I'd choose:

- ❏ Novel
- ❏ Short story collection
- ❏ Mystery
- ❏ Adventure
- ☑ Romance
- ❏ Science fiction
- ❏ Fairy tale
- ❏ Nonfiction
- ❏ Travel
- ❏ Other: ....

And here's why: I've always liked and read romance novels and thought that they were really cute and different from real life and gave people hope about finding the one. Because usually when you watch t.v. it shows you how sex-craved people can be and I'd want to tell people that there are others not like that ☺ Thank god

Me, My Friends,
and Books

Here's a list of my favorite friends and their favorite books!

MY FRIEND: May LaFlamme

FAVORITE BOOK: Burned

WHY THEY LIKE IT: Interesting and about drugs

HAVE I READ IT YET? Nope.

MY FRIEND: Ashley Baldwin

FAVORITE BOOK: Twisted

WHY THEY LIKE IT: funny and misterious

HAVE I READ IT YET? Yes, I recommended it :)

MY FRIEND: Dayna Carlson

FAVORITE BOOK: The Uglies

WHY THEY LIKE IT: Adventurous + action

HAVE I READ IT YET? yes :)

MY FRIEND:

FAVORITE BOOK:

WHY THEY LIKE IT:

HAVE I READ IT YET?

MY FRIEND: ....

FAVORITE BOOK: ....

WHY THEY LIKE IT: ....

HAVE I READ IT YET? ....

MY FRIEND: ....

FAVORITE BOOK: ....

WHY THEY LIKE IT: ....

HAVE I READ IT YET? ....

MY FRIEND: ....

FAVORITE BOOK: ....

WHY THEY LIKE IT: ....

HAVE I READ IT YET? ....

MY FRIEND: ....

FAVORITE BOOK: ....

WHY THEY LIKE IT: ....

HAVE I READ IT YET? ....

Here's a list of my favorite friends and their favorite books!

MY FRIEND: ....

FAVORITE BOOK: ....

WHY THEY LIKE IT: ....

HAVE I READ IT YET? ....

MY FRIEND: ....

FAVORITE BOOK: ....

WHY THEY LIKE IT: ....

HAVE I READ IT YET? ....

MY FRIEND: ....

FAVORITE BOOK: ....

WHY THEY LIKE IT: ....

HAVE I READ IT YET? ....

MY FRIEND: ....

FAVORITE BOOK: ....

WHY THEY LIKE IT: ....

HAVE I READ IT YET? ....

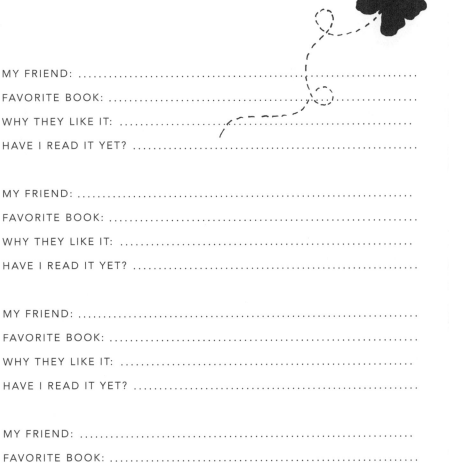

MY FRIEND: ....

FAVORITE BOOK: ....

WHY THEY LIKE IT: ....

HAVE I READ IT YET? ....

MY FRIEND: ....

FAVORITE BOOK: ....

WHY THEY LIKE IT: ....

HAVE I READ IT YET? ....

MY FRIEND: ....

FAVORITE BOOK: ....

WHY THEY LIKE IT: ....

HAVE I READ IT YET? ....

MY FRIEND: ....

FAVORITE BOOK: ....

WHY THEY LIKE IT: ....

HAVE I READ IT YET? ....

Here's a list of my favorite friends and their favorite books!

MY FRIEND: ....

FAVORITE BOOK: ....

WHY THEY LIKE IT: ....

HAVE I READ IT YET? ....

MY FRIEND: ....

FAVORITE BOOK: ....

WHY THEY LIKE IT: ....

HAVE I READ IT YET? ....

MY FRIEND: ....

FAVORITE BOOK: ....

WHY THEY LIKE IT: ....

HAVE I READ IT YET? ....

MY FRIEND: ....

FAVORITE BOOK: ....

WHY THEY LIKE IT: ....

HAVE I READ IT YET? ....

MY FRIEND: ....

FAVORITE BOOK: ....

WHY THEY LIKE IT: ....

HAVE I READ IT YET? ....

MY FRIEND: ....

FAVORITE BOOK: ....

WHY THEY LIKE IT: ....

HAVE I READ IT YET? ....

MY FRIEND: ....

FAVORITE BOOK: ....

WHY THEY LIKE IT: ....

HAVE I READ IT YET? ....

MY FRIEND: ....

FAVORITE BOOK: ....

WHY THEY LIKE IT: ....

HAVE I READ IT YET? ....

Here's a list of my favorite friends and their favorite books!

MY FRIEND: ....

FAVORITE BOOK: ....

WHY THEY LIKE IT: ....

HAVE I READ IT YET? ....

MY FRIEND: ....

FAVORITE BOOK: ....

WHY THEY LIKE IT: ....

HAVE I READ IT YET? ....

MY FRIEND: ....

FAVORITE BOOK: ....

WHY THEY LIKE IT: ....

HAVE I READ IT YET? ....

MY FRIEND: ....

FAVORITE BOOK: ....

WHY THEY LIKE IT: ....

HAVE I READ IT YET? ....

MY FRIEND: ....

FAVORITE BOOK: ....

WHY THEY LIKE IT: ....

HAVE I READ IT YET? ....

MY FRIEND: ....

FAVORITE BOOK: ....

WHY THEY LIKE IT: ....

HAVE I READ IT YET? ....

MY FRIEND: ....

FAVORITE BOOK: ....

WHY THEY LIKE IT: ....

HAVE I READ IT YET? ....

MY FRIEND: ....

FAVORITE BOOK: ....

WHY THEY LIKE IT: ....

HAVE I READ IT YET? ....

Here's a list of my favorite friends and their favorite books!

MY FRIEND: ....

FAVORITE BOOK: ....

WHY THEY LIKE IT: ....

HAVE I READ IT YET? ....

MY FRIEND: ....

FAVORITE BOOK: ....

WHY THEY LIKE IT: ....

HAVE I READ IT YET? ....

MY FRIEND: ....

FAVORITE BOOK: ....

WHY THEY LIKE IT: ....

HAVE I READ IT YET? ....

MY FRIEND: ....

FAVORITE BOOK: ....

WHY THEY LIKE IT: ....

HAVE I READ IT YET? ....

MY FRIEND: ....

FAVORITE BOOK: ....

WHY THEY LIKE IT: ....

HAVE I READ IT YET? ....

MY FRIEND: ....

FAVORITE BOOK: ....

WHY THEY LIKE IT: ....

HAVE I READ IT YET? ....

MY FRIEND: ....

FAVORITE BOOK: ....

WHY THEY LIKE IT: ....

HAVE I READ IT YET? ....

MY FRIEND: ....

FAVORITE BOOK: ....

WHY THEY LIKE IT: ....

HAVE I READ IT YET? ....

Here are the books that people in my family especially love:

NAME: ....

FAVORITE BOOK: ....

WHY THEY LIKE IT: ....

HAVE I READ IT YET? ....

NAME: ....

FAVORITE BOOK: ....

WHY THEY LIKE IT: ....

HAVE I READ IT YET? ....

NAME: ....

FAVORITE BOOK: ....

WHY THEY LIKE IT: ....

HAVE I READ IT YET? ....

NAME: ....

FAVORITE BOOK: ....

WHY THEY LIKE IT: ....

HAVE I READ IT YET? ....

NAME: ....

FAVORITE BOOK: ....

WHY THEY LIKE IT: ....

HAVE I READ IT YET? ....

NAME: ....

FAVORITE BOOK: ....

WHY THEY LIKE IT: ....

HAVE I READ IT YET? ....

NAME: ....

FAVORITE BOOK: ....

WHY THEY LIKE IT: ....

HAVE I READ IT YET? ....

NAME: ....

FAVORITE BOOK: ....

WHY THEY LIKE IT: ....

HAVE I READ IT YET? ....

Here are the books that people in my family especially love:

NAME: ....

FAVORITE BOOK: ....

WHY THEY LIKE IT: ....

HAVE I READ IT YET? ....

NAME: ....

FAVORITE BOOK: ....

WHY THEY LIKE IT: ....

HAVE I READ IT YET? ....

NAME: ....

FAVORITE BOOK: ....

WHY THEY LIKE IT: ....

HAVE I READ IT YET? ....

NAME: ....

FAVORITE BOOK: ....

WHY THEY LIKE IT: ....

HAVE I READ IT YET? ....

NAME: ....

FAVORITE BOOK: ....

WHY THEY LIKE IT: ....

HAVE I READ IT YET? ....

NAME: ....

FAVORITE BOOK: ....

WHY THEY LIKE IT: ....

HAVE I READ IT YET? ....

NAME: ....

FAVORITE BOOK: ....

WHY THEY LIKE IT: ....

HAVE I READ IT YET? ....

NAME: ....

FAVORITE BOOK: ....

WHY THEY LIKE IT: ....

HAVE I READ IT YET? ....

Here are the books that people in my family especially love:

NAME: ....

FAVORITE BOOK: ....

WHY THEY LIKE IT: ....

HAVE I READ IT YET? ....

NAME: ....

FAVORITE BOOK: ....

WHY THEY LIKE IT: ....

HAVE I READ IT YET? ....

NAME: ....

FAVORITE BOOK: ....

WHY THEY LIKE IT: ....

HAVE I READ IT YET? ....

NAME: ....

FAVORITE BOOK: ....

WHY THEY LIKE IT: ....

HAVE I READ IT YET? ....

NAME: ....

FAVORITE BOOK: ....

WHY THEY LIKE IT: ....

HAVE I READ IT YET? ....

NAME: ....

FAVORITE BOOK: ....

WHY THEY LIKE IT: ....

HAVE I READ IT YET? ....

NAME: ....

FAVORITE BOOK: ....

WHY THEY LIKE IT: ....

HAVE I READ IT YET? ....

NAME: ....

FAVORITE BOOK: ....

WHY THEY LIKE IT: ....

HAVE I READ IT YET? ....

Here are the books that people in my family especially love:

NAME: ....

FAVORITE BOOK: ....

WHY THEY LIKE IT: ....

HAVE I READ IT YET? ....

NAME: ....

FAVORITE BOOK: ....

WHY THEY LIKE IT: ....

HAVE I READ IT YET? ....

NAME: ....

FAVORITE BOOK: ....

WHY THEY LIKE IT: ....

HAVE I READ IT YET? ....

NAME: ....

FAVORITE BOOK: ....

WHY THEY LIKE IT: ....

HAVE I READ IT YET? ....

NAME: ....

FAVORITE BOOK: ....

WHY THEY LIKE IT: ....

HAVE I READ IT YET? ....

NAME: ....

FAVORITE BOOK: ....

WHY THEY LIKE IT: ....

HAVE I READ IT YET? ....

NAME: ....

FAVORITE BOOK: ....

WHY THEY LIKE IT: ....

HAVE I READ IT YET? ....

NAME: ....

FAVORITE BOOK: ....

WHY THEY LIKE IT: ....

HAVE I READ IT YET? ....

What books did my parents like best when they were my age?

MOM

1. ....

2. ....

3. ....

4. ....

5. ....

DAD

1. ....

2. ....

3. ....

4. ....

5. ....

My Book Club

Check out the books my friends and I have been reading!

TITLE: ...... Twisted ....

AUTHOR: ....

INITIALS:	RATING:			
AB	☑ Loved it!	❑ Liked it!	❑ Just okay	❑ Not my thing
II	☑ Loved it!	❑ Liked it!	❑ Just okay	❑ Not my thing
....	❑ Loved it!	❑ Liked it!	❑ Just okay	❑ Not my thing
....	❑ Loved it!	❑ Liked it!	❑ Just okay	❑ Not my thing
....	❑ Loved it!	❑ Liked it!	❑ Just okay	❑ Not my thing
....	❑ Loved it!	❑ Liked it!	❑ Just okay	❑ Not my thing
....	❑ Loved it!	❑ Liked it!	❑ Just okay	❑ Not my thing
....	❑ Loved it!	❑ Liked it!	❑ Just okay	❑ Not my thing
....	❑ Loved it!	❑ Liked it!	❑ Just okay	❑ Not my thing
....	❑ Loved it!	❑ Liked it!	❑ Just okay	❑ Not my thing
....	❑ Loved it!	❑ Liked it!	❑ Just okay	❑ Not my thing
....	❑ Loved it!	❑ Liked it!	❑ Just okay	❑ Not my thing
....	❑ Loved it!	❑ Liked it!	❑ Just okay	❑ Not my thing
....	❑ Loved it!	❑ Liked it!	❑ Just okay	❑ Not my thing
....	❑ Loved it!	❑ Liked it!	❑ Just okay	❑ Not my thing
....	❑ Loved it!	❑ Liked it!	❑ Just okay	❑ Not my thing
....	❑ Loved it!	❑ Liked it!	❑ Just okay	❑ Not my thing

TITLE: ...Twilight.....................................

AUTHOR: ...Stephanie...Meyer.....................

INITIALS:	RATING:			
I.I.	☑ Loved it!	❏ Liked it!	❏ Just okay	❏ Not my thing
DC	☑ Loved it!	❏ Liked it!	❏ Just okay	❏ Not my thing
ML	❏ Loved it!	❏ Liked it!	❏ Just okay	☑ Not my thing
AB	☑ Loved it!	❏ Liked it!	❏ Just okay	❏ Not my thing
SL	❏ Loved it!	❏ Liked it!	☑ Just okay	❏ Not my thing
....	❏ Loved it!	❏ Liked it!	❏ Just okay	❏ Not my thing
....	❏ Loved it!	❏ Liked it!	❏ Just okay	❏ Not my thing
....	❏ Loved it!	❏ Liked it!	❏ Just okay	❏ Not my thing
....	❏ Loved it!	❏ Liked it!	❏ Just okay	❏ Not my thing
....	❏ Loved it!	❏ Liked it!	❏ Just okay	❏ Not my thing
....	❏ Loved it!	❏ Liked it!	❏ Just okay	❏ Not my thing
....	❏ Loved it!	❏ Liked it!	❏ Just okay	❏ Not my thing
....	❏ Loved it!	❏ Liked it!	❏ Just okay	❏ Not my thing
....	❏ Loved it!	❏ Liked it!	❏ Just okay	❏ Not my thing
....	❏ Loved it!	❏ Liked it!	❏ Just okay	❏ Not my thing
....	❏ Loved it!	❏ Liked it!	❏ Just okay	❏ Not my thing
....	❏ Loved it!	❏ Liked it!	❏ Just okay	❏ Not my thing

Check out the books my friends and I have been reading!

TITLE: ....

AUTHOR: ....

INITIALS: RATING:

....   ❑ Loved it!   ❑ Liked it!   ❑ Just okay   ❑ Not my thing

....   ❑ Loved it!   ❑ Liked it!   ❑ Just okay   ❑ Not my thing

....   ❑ Loved it!   ❑ Liked it!   ❑ Just okay   ❑ Not my thing

....   ❑ Loved it!   ❑ Liked it!   ❑ Just okay   ❑ Not my thing

....   ❑ Loved it!   ❑ Liked it!   ❑ Just okay   ❑ Not my thing

....   ❑ Loved it!   ❑ Liked it!   ❑ Just okay   ❑ Not my thing

....   ❑ Loved it!   ❑ Liked it!   ❑ Just okay   ❑ Not my thing

....   ❑ Loved it!   ❑ Liked it!   ❑ Just okay   ❑ Not my thing

....   ❑ Loved it!   ❑ Liked it!   ❑ Just okay   ❑ Not my thing

....   ❑ Loved it!   ❑ Liked it!   ❑ Just okay   ❑ Not my thing

....   ❑ Loved it!   ❑ Liked it!   ❑ Just okay   ❑ Not my thing

....   ❑ Loved it!   ❑ Liked it!   ❑ Just okay   ❑ Not my thing

....   ❑ Loved it!   ❑ Liked it!   ❑ Just okay   ❑ Not my thing

....   ❑ Loved it!   ❑ Liked it!   ❑ Just okay   ❑ Not my thing

....   ❑ Loved it!   ❑ Liked it!   ❑ Just okay   ❑ Not my thing

....   ❑ Loved it!   ❑ Liked it!   ❑ Just okay   ❑ Not my thing

TITLE: ....

AUTHOR: ....

INITIALS: RATING:

....	❑ Loved it!	❑ Liked it!	❑ Just okay	❑ Not my thing
....	❑ Loved it!	❑ Liked it!	❑ Just okay	❑ Not my thing
....	❑ Loved it!	❑ Liked it!	❑ Just okay	❑ Not my thing
....	❑ Loved it!	❑ Liked it!	❑ Just okay	❑ Not my thing
....	❑ Loved it!	❑ Liked it!	❑ Just okay	❑ Not my thing
....	❑ Loved it!	❑ Liked it!	❑ Just okay	❑ Not my thing
....	❑ Loved it!	❑ Liked it!	❑ Just okay	❑ Not my thing
....	❑ Loved it!	❑ Liked it!	❑ Just okay	❑ Not my thing
....	❑ Loved it!	❑ Liked it!	❑ Just okay	❑ Not my thing
....	❑ Loved it!	❑ Liked it!	❑ Just okay	❑ Not my thing
....	❑ Loved it!	❑ Liked it!	❑ Just okay	❑ Not my thing
....	❑ Loved it!	❑ Liked it!	❑ Just okay	❑ Not my thing
....	❑ Loved it!	❑ Liked it!	❑ Just okay	❑ Not my thing
....	❑ Loved it!	❑ Liked it!	❑ Just okay	❑ Not my thing
....	❑ Loved it!	❑ Liked it!	❑ Just okay	❑ Not my thing
....	❑ Loved it!	❑ Liked it!	❑ Just okay	❑ Not my thing
....	❑ Loved it!	❑ Liked it!	❑ Just okay	❑ Not my thing
....	❑ Loved it!	❑ Liked it!	❑ Just okay	❑ Not my thing

Check out the books my friends and I have been reading!

TITLE: ....

AUTHOR: ....

INITIALS: RATING:

....   ❑ Loved it!   ❑ Liked it!   ❑ Just okay   ❑ Not my thing

....   ❑ Loved it!   ❑ Liked it!   ❑ Just okay   ❑ Not my thing

....   ❑ Loved it!   ❑ Liked it!   ❑ Just okay   ❑ Not my thing

....   ❑ Loved it!   ❑ Liked it!   ❑ Just okay   ❑ Not my thing

....   ❑ Loved it!   ❑ Liked it!   ❑ Just okay   ❑ Not my thing

....   ❑ Loved it!   ❑ Liked it!   ❑ Just okay   ❑ Not my thing

....   ❑ Loved it!   ❑ Liked it!   ❑ Just okay   ❑ Not my thing

....   ❑ Loved it!   ❑ Liked it!   ❑ Just okay   ❑ Not my thing

....   ❑ Loved it!   ❑ Liked it!   ❑ Just okay   ❑ Not my thing

....   ❑ Loved it!   ❑ Liked it!   ❑ Just okay   ❑ Not my thing

....   ❑ Loved it!   ❑ Liked it!   ❑ Just okay   ❑ Not my thing

....   ❑ Loved it!   ❑ Liked it!   ❑ Just okay   ❑ Not my thing

....   ❑ Loved it!   ❑ Liked it!   ❑ Just okay   ❑ Not my thing

....   ❑ Loved it!   ❑ Liked it!   ❑ Just okay   ❑ Not my thing

....   ❑ Loved it!   ❑ Liked it!   ❑ Just okay   ❑ Not my thing

....   ❑ Loved it!   ❑ Liked it!   ❑ Just okay   ❑ Not my thing

....   ❑ Loved it!   ❑ Liked it!   ❑ Just okay   ❑ Not my thing

TITLE: ....

AUTHOR: ....

INITIALS: RATING:

....   ❏ Loved it!   ❏ Liked it!   ❏ Just okay   ❏ Not my thing

....   ❏ Loved it!   ❏ Liked it!   ❏ Just okay   ❏ Not my thing

....   ❏ Loved it!   ❏ Liked it!   ❏ Just okay   ❏ Not my thing

....   ❏ Loved it!   ❏ Liked it!   ❏ Just okay   ❏ Not my thing

....   ❏ Loved it!   ❏ Liked it!   ❏ Just okay   ❏ Not my thing

....   ❏ Loved it!   ❏ Liked it!   ❏ Just okay   ❏ Not my thing

....   ❏ Loved it!   ❏ Liked it!   ❏ Just okay   ❏ Not my thing

....   ❏ Loved it!   ❏ Liked it!   ❏ Just okay   ❏ Not my thing

....   ❏ Loved it!   ❏ Liked it!   ❏ Just okay   ❏ Not my thing

....   ❏ Loved it!   ❏ Liked it!   ❏ Just okay   ❏ Not my thing

....   ❏ Loved it!   ❏ Liked it!   ❏ Just okay   ❏ Not my thing

....   ❏ Loved it!   ❏ Liked it!   ❏ Just okay   ❏ Not my thing

....   ❏ Loved it!   ❏ Liked it!   ❏ Just okay   ❏ Not my thing

....   ❏ Loved it!   ❏ Liked it!   ❏ Just okay   ❏ Not my thing

....   ❏ Loved it!   ❏ Liked it!   ❏ Just okay   ❏ Not my thing

....   ❏ Loved it!   ❏ Liked it!   ❏ Just okay   ❏ Not my thing

....   ❏ Loved it!   ❏ Liked it!   ❏ Just okay   ❏ Not my thing

Check out the books my friends and I have been reading!

TITLE: ....

AUTHOR: ....

INITIALS: RATING:

....   ❏ Loved it!   ❏ Liked it!   ❏ Just okay   ❏ Not my thing

....   ❏ Loved it!   ❏ Liked it!   ❏ Just okay   ❏ Not my thing

....   ❏ Loved it!   ❏ Liked it!   ❏ Just okay   ❏ Not my thing

....   ❏ Loved it!   ❏ Liked it!   ❏ Just okay   ❏ Not my thing

....   ❏ Loved it!   ❏ Liked it!   ❏ Just okay   ❏ Not my thing

....   ❏ Loved it!   ❏ Liked it!   ❏ Just okay   ❏ Not my thing

....   ❏ Loved it!   ❏ Liked it!   ❏ Just okay   ❏ Not my thing

....   ❏ Loved it!   ❏ Liked it!   ❏ Just okay   ❏ Not my thing

....   ❏ Loved it!   ❏ Liked it!   ❏ Just okay   ❏ Not my thing

....   ❏ Loved it!   ❏ Liked it!   ❏ Just okay   ❏ Not my thing

....   ❏ Loved it!   ❏ Liked it!   ❏ Just okay   ❏ Not my thing

....   ❏ Loved it!   ❏ Liked it!   ❏ Just okay   ❏ Not my thing

....   ❏ Loved it!   ❏ Liked it!   ❏ Just okay   ❏ Not my thing

....   ❏ Loved it!   ❏ Liked it!   ❏ Just okay   ❏ Not my thing

....   ❏ Loved it!   ❏ Liked it!   ❏ Just okay   ❏ Not my thing

....   ❏ Loved it!   ❏ Liked it!   ❏ Just okay   ❏ Not my thing

....   ❏ Loved it!   ❏ Liked it!   ❏ Just okay   ❏ Not my thing

TITLE: ....

AUTHOR: ....

INITIALS: RATING:

....   ❑ Loved it!   ❑ Liked it!   ❑ Just okay   ❑ Not my thing

....   ❑ Loved it!   ❑ Liked it!   ❑ Just okay   ❑ Not my thing

....   ❑ Loved it!   ❑ Liked it!   ❑ Just okay   ❑ Not my thing

....   ❑ Loved it!   ❑ Liked it!   ❑ Just okay   ❑ Not my thing

....   ❑ Loved it!   ❑ Liked it!   ❑ Just okay   ❑ Not my thing

....   ❑ Loved it!   ❑ Liked it!   ❑ Just okay   ❑ Not my thing

....   ❑ Loved it!   ❑ Liked it!   ❑ Just okay   ❑ Not my thing

....   ❑ Loved it!   ❑ Liked it!   ❑ Just okay   ❑ Not my thing

....   ❑ Loved it!   ❑ Liked it!   ❑ Just okay   ❑ Not my thing

....   ❑ Loved it!   ❑ Liked it!   ❑ Just okay   ❑ Not my thing

....   ❑ Loved it!   ❑ Liked it!   ❑ Just okay   ❑. Not my thing

....   ❑ Loved it!   ❑ Liked it!   ❑ Just okay   ❑ Not my thing

....   ❑ Loved it!   ❑ Liked it!   ❑ Just okay   ❑ Not my thing

....   ❑ Loved it!   ❑ Liked it!   ❑ Just okay   ❑ Not my thing

....   ❑ Loved it!   ❑ Liked it!   ❑ Just okay   ❑ Not my thing

....   ❑ Loved it!   ❑ Liked it!   ❑ Just okay   ❑ Not my thing

....   ❑ Loved it!   ❑ Liked it!   ❑ Just okay   ❑ Not my thing

Check out the books my friends and I have been reading!

TITLE: ....

AUTHOR: ....

INITIALS: RATING:

....	❑ Loved it!	❑ Liked it!	❑ Just okay	❑ Not my thing
....	❑ Loved it!	❑ Liked it!	❑ Just okay	❑ Not my thing
....	❑ Loved it!	❑ Liked it!	❑ Just okay	❑ Not my thing
....	❑ Loved it!	❑ Liked it!	❑ Just okay	❑ Not my thing
....	❑ Loved it!	❑ Liked it!	❑ Just okay	❑ Not my thing
....	❑ Loved it!	❑ Liked it!	❑ Just okay	❑ Not my thing
....	❑ Loved it!	❑ Liked it!	❑ Just okay	❑ Not my thing
....	❑ Loved it!	❑ Liked it!	❑ Just okay	❑ Not my thing
....	❑ Loved it!	❑ Liked it!	❑ Just okay	❑ Not my thing
....	❑ Loved it!	❑ Liked it!	❑ Just okay	❑ Not my thing
....	❑ Loved it!	❑ Liked it!	❑ Just okay	❑ Not my thing
....	❑ Loved it!	❑ Liked it!	❑ Just okay	❑ Not my thing
....	❑ Loved it!	❑ Liked it!	❑ Just okay	❑ Not my thing
....	❑ Loved it!	❑ Liked it!	❑ Just okay	❑ Not my thing
....	❑ Loved it!	❑ Liked it!	❑ Just okay	❑ Not my thing
....	❑ Loved it!	❑ Liked it!	❑ Just okay	❑ Not my thing
....	❑ Loved it!	❑ Liked it!	❑ Just okay	❑ Not my thing

TITLE: ....

AUTHOR: ....

INITIALS: RATING:

.... ❑ Loved it!   ❑ Liked it!   ❑ Just okay   ❑ Not my thing

.... ❑ Loved it!   ❑ Liked it!   ❑ Just okay   ❑ Not my thing

.... ❑ Loved it!   ❑ Liked it!   ❑ Just okay   ❑ Not my thing

.... ❑ Loved it!   ❑ Liked it!   ❑ Just okay   ❑ Not my thing

.... ❑ Loved it!   ❑ Liked it!   ❑ Just okay   ❑ Not my thing

.... ❑ Loved it!   ❑ Liked it!   ❑ Just okay   ❑ Not my thing

.... ❑ Loved it!   ❑ Liked it!   ❑ Just okay   ❑ Not my thing

.... ❑ Loved it!   ❑ Liked it!   ❑ Just okay   ❑ Not my thing

.... ❑ Loved it!   ❑ Liked it!   ❑ Just okay   ❑ Not my thing

.... ❑ Loved it!   ❑ Liked it!   ❑ Just okay   ❑ Not my thing

.... ❑ Loved it!   ❑ Liked it!   ❑ Just okay   ❑ Not my thing

.... ❑ Loved it!   ❑ Liked it!   ❑ Just okay   ❑ Not my thing

.... ❑ Loved it!   ❑ Liked it!   ❑ Just okay   ❑ Not my thing

.... ❑ Loved it!   ❑ Liked it!   ❑ Just okay   ❑ Not my thing

.... ❑ Loved it!   ❑ Liked it!   ❑ Just okay   ❑ Not my thing

.... ❑ Loved it!   ❑ Liked it!   ❑ Just okay   ❑ Not my thing

.... ❑ Loved it!   ❑ Liked it!   ❑ Just okay   ❑ Not my thing

Check out the books my friends and I have been reading!

TITLE: ....

AUTHOR: ....

INITIALS: RATING:

....   ❑ Loved it!   ❑ Liked it!   ❑ Just okay   ❑ Not my thing

....   ❑ Loved it!   ❑ Liked it!   ❑ Just okay   ❑ Not my thing

....   ❑ Loved it!   ❑ Liked it!   ❑ Just okay   ❑ Not my thing

....   ❑ Loved it!   ❑ Liked it!   ❑ Just okay   ❑ Not my thing

....   ❑ Loved it!   ❑ Liked it!   ❑ Just okay   ❑ Not my thing

....   ❑ Loved it!   ❑ Liked it!   ❑ Just okay   ❑ Not my thing

....   ❑ Loved it!   ❑ Liked it!   ❑ Just okay   ❑ Not my thing

....   ❑ Loved it!   ❑ Liked it!   ❑ Just okay   ❑ Not my thing

....   ❑ Loved it!   ❑ Liked it!   ❑ Just okay   ❑ Not my thing

....   ❑ Loved it!   ❑ Liked it!   ❑ Just okay   ❑ Not my thing

....   ❑ Loved it!   ❑ Liked it!   ❑ Just okay   ❑ Not my thing

....   ❑ Loved it!   ❑ Liked it!   ❑ Just okay   ❑ Not my thing

....   ❑ Loved it!   ❑ Liked it!   ❑ Just okay   ❑ Not my thing

....   ❑ Loved it!   ❑ Liked it!   ❑ Just okay   ❑ Not my thing

....   ❑ Loved it!   ❑ Liked it!   ❑ Just okay   ❑ Not my thing

....   ❑ Loved it!   ❑ Liked it!   ❑ Just okay   ❑ Not my thing

....   ❑ Loved it!   ❑ Liked it!   ❑ Just okay   ❑ Not my thing

TITLE: ....

AUTHOR: ....

INITIALS: RATING:

.... ❑ Loved it! ❑ Liked it! ❑ Just okay ❑ Not my thing

.... ❑ Loved it! ❑ Liked it! ❑ Just okay ❑ Not my thing

.... ❑ Loved it! ❑ Liked it! ❑ Just okay ❑ Not my thing

.... ❑ Loved it! ❑ Liked it! ❑ Just okay ❑ Not my thing

.... ❑ Loved it! ❑ Liked it! ❑ Just okay ❑ Not my thing

.... ❑ Loved it! ❑ Liked it! ❑ Just okay ❑ Not my thing

.... ❑ Loved it! ❑ Liked it! ❑ Just okay ❑ Not my thing

.... ❑ Loved it! ❑ Liked it! ❑ Just okay ❑ Not my thing

.... ❑ Loved it! ❑ Liked it! ❑ Just okay ❑ Not my thing

.... ❑ Loved it! ❑ Liked it! ❑ Just okay ❑ Not my thing

.... ❑ Loved it! ❑ Liked it! ❑ Just okay ❑ Not my thing

.... ❑ Loved it! ❑ Liked it! ❑ Just okay ❑ Not my thing

.... ❑ Loved it! ❑ Liked it! ❑ Just okay ❑ Not my thing

.... ❑ Loved it! ❑ Liked it! ❑ Just okay ❑ Not my thing

.... ❑ Loved it! ❑ Liked it! ❑ Just okay ❑ Not my thing

.... ❑ Loved it! ❑ Liked it! ❑ Just okay ❑ Not my thing

.... ❑ Loved it! ❑ Liked it! ❑ Just okay ❑ Not my thing

Check out the books my friends and I have been reading!

TITLE: ....

AUTHOR: ....

INITIALS: RATING:

....   ❏ Loved it!   ❏ Liked it!   ❏ Just okay   ❏ Not my thing

....   ❏ Loved it!   ❏ Liked it!   ❏ Just okay   ❏ Not my thing

....   ❏ Loved it!   ❏ Liked it!   ❏ Just okay   ❏ Not my thing

....   ❏ Loved it!   ❏ Liked it!   ❏ Just okay   ❏ Not my thing

....   ❏ Loved it!   ❏ Liked it!   ❏ Just okay   ❏ Not my thing

....   ❏ Loved it!   ❏ Liked it!   ❏ Just okay   ❏ Not my thing

....   ❏ Loved it!   ❏ Liked it!   ❏ Just okay   ❏ Not my thing

....   ❏ Loved it!   ❏ Liked it!   ❏ Just okay   ❏ Not my thing

....   ❏ Loved it!   ❏ Liked it!   ❏ Just okay   ❏ Not my thing

....   ❏ Loved it!   ❏ Liked it!   ❏ Just okay   ❏ Not my thing

....   ❏ Loved it!   ❏ Liked it!   ❏ Just okay   ❏ Not my thing

....   ❏ Loved it!   ❏ Liked it!   ❏ Just okay   ❏ Not my thing

....   ❏ Loved it!   ❏ Liked it!   ❏ Just okay   ❏ Not my thing

....   ❏ Loved it!   ❏ Liked it!   ❏ Just okay   ❏ Not my thing

....   ❏ Loved it!   ❏ Liked it!   ❏ Just okay   ❏ Not my thing

....   ❏ Loved it!   ❏ Liked it!   ❏ Just okay   ❏ Not my thing

....   ❏ Loved it!   ❏ Liked it!   ❏ Just okay   ❏ Not my thing

TITLE: ....

AUTHOR: ....

INITIALS: RATING:

....   ☐ Loved it!   ☐ Liked it!   ☐ Just okay   ☐ Not my thing

....   ☐ Loved it!   ☐ Liked it!   ☐ Just okay   ☐ Not my thing

....   ☐ Loved it!   ☐ Liked it!   ☐ Just okay   ☐ Not my thing

....   ☐ Loved it!   ☐ Liked it!   ☐ Just okay   ☐ Not my thing

....   ☐ Loved it!   ☐ Liked it!   ☐ Just okay   ☐ Not my thing

....   ☐ Loved it!   ☐ Liked it!   ☐ Just okay   ☐ Not my thing

....   ☐ Loved it!   ☐ Liked it!   ☐ Just okay   ☐ Not my thing

....   ☐ Loved it!   ☐ Liked it!   ☐ Just okay   ☐ Not my thing

....   ☐ Loved it!   ☐ Liked it!   ☐ Just okay   ☐ Not my thing

....   ☐ Loved it!   ☐ Liked it!   ☐ Just okay   ☐ Not my thing

....   ☐ Loved it!   ☐ Liked it!   ☐ Just okay   ☐ Not my thing

....   ☐ Loved it!   ☐ Liked it!   ☐ Just okay   ☐ Not my thing

....   ☐ Loved it!   ☐ Liked it!   ☐ Just okay   ☐ Not my thing

....   ☐ Loved it!   ☐ Liked it!   ☐ Just okay   ☐ Not my thing

....   ☐ Loved it!   ☐ Liked it!   ☐ Just okay   ☐ Not my thing

....   ☐ Loved it!   ☐ Liked it!   ☐ Just okay   ☐ Not my thing

....   ☐ Loved it!   ☐ Liked it!   ☐ Just okay   ☐ Not my thing

Check out the books my friends and I have been reading!

TITLE: ....

AUTHOR: ....

INITIALS: RATING:

.... ❑ Loved it! ❑ Liked it! ❑ Just okay ❑ Not my thing

.... ❑ Loved it! ❑ Liked it! ❑ Just okay ❑ Not my thing

.... ❑ Loved it! ❑ Liked it! ❑ Just okay ❑ Not my thing

.... ❑ Loved it! ❑ Liked it! ❑ Just okay ❑ Not my thing

.... ❑ Loved it! ❑ Liked it! ❑ Just okay ❑ Not my thing

.... ❑ Loved it! ❑ Liked it! ❑ Just okay ❑ Not my thing

.... ❑ Loved it! ❑ Liked it! ❑ Just okay ❑ Not my thing

.... ❑ Loved it! ❑ Liked it! ❑ Just okay ❑ Not my thing

.... ❑ Loved it! ❑ Liked it! ❑ Just okay ❑ Not my thing

.... ❑ Loved it! ❑ Liked it! ❑ Just okay ❑ Not my thing

.... ❑ Loved it! ❑ Liked it! ❑ Just okay ❑ Not my thing

.... ❑ Loved it! ❑ Liked it! ❑ Just okay ❑ Not my thing

.... ❑ Loved it! ❑ Liked it! ❑ Just okay ❑ Not my thing

.... ❑ Loved it! ❑ Liked it! ❑ Just okay ❑ Not my thing

.... ❑ Loved it! ❑ Liked it! ❑ Just okay ❑ Not my thing

.... ❑ Loved it! ❑ Liked it! ❑ Just okay ❑ Not my thing

.... ❑ Loved it! ❑ Liked it! ❑ Just okay ❑ Not my thing

TITLE: ....

AUTHOR: ....

INITIALS:	RATING:			
....	❑ Loved it!	❑ Liked it!	❑ Just okay	❑ Not my thing
....	❑ Loved it!	❑ Liked it!	❑ Just okay	❑ Not my thing
....	❑ Loved it!	❑ Liked it!	❑ Just okay	❑ Not my thing
....	❑ Loved it!	❑ Liked it!	❑ Just okay	❑ Not my thing
....	❑ Loved it!	❑ Liked it!	❑ Just okay	❑ Not my thing
....	❑ Loved it!	❑ Liked it!	❑ Just okay	❑ Not my thing
....	❑ Loved it!	❑ Liked it!	❑ Just okay	❑ Not my thing
....	❑ Loved it!	❑ Liked it!	❑ Just okay	❑ Not my thing
....	❑ Loved it!	❑ Liked it!	❑ Just okay	❑ Not my thing
....	❑ Loved it!	❑ Liked it!	❑ Just okay	❑ Not my thing
....	❑ Loved it!	❑ Liked it!	❑ Just okay	❑ Not my thing
....	❑ Loved it!	❑ Liked it!	❑ Just okay	❑ Not my thing
....	❑ Loved it!	❑ Liked it!	❑ Just okay	❑ Not my thing
....	❑ Loved it!	❑ Liked it!	❑ Just okay	❑ Not my thing
....	❑ Loved it!	❑ Liked it!	❑ Just okay	❑ Not my thing
....	❑ Loved it!	❑ Liked it!	❑ Just okay	❑ Not my thing
....	❑ Loved it!	❑ Liked it!	❑ Just okay	❑ Not my thing

Check out the books my friends and I have been reading!

TITLE: ....

AUTHOR: ....

INITIALS: RATING:

....   ❑ Loved it!   ❑ Liked it!   ❑ Just okay   ❑ Not my thing

....   ❑ Loved it!   ❑ Liked it!   ❑ Just okay   ❑ Not my thing

....   ❑ Loved it!   ❑ Liked it!   ❑ Just okay   ❑ Not my thing

....   ❑ Loved it!   ❑ Liked it!   ❑ Just okay   ❑ Not my thing

....   ❑ Loved it!   ❑ Liked it!   ❑ Just okay   ❑ Not my thing

....   ❑ Loved it!   ❑ Liked it!   ❑ Just okay   ❑ Not my thing

....   ❑ Loved it!   ❑ Liked it!   ❑ Just okay   ❑ Not my thing

....   ❑ Loved it!   ❑ Liked it!   ❑ Just okay   ❑ Not my thing

....   ❑ Loved it!   ❑ Liked it!   ❑ Just okay   ❑ Not my thing

....   ❑ Loved it!   ❑ Liked it!   ❑ Just okay   ❑ Not my thing

....   ❑ Loved it!   ❑ Liked it!   ❑ Just okay   ❑ Not my thing

....   ❑ Loved it!   ❑ Liked it!   ❑ Just okay   ❑ Not my thing

....   ❑ Loved it!   ❑ Liked it!   ❑ Just okay   ❑ Not my thing

....   ❑ Loved it!   ❑ Liked it!   ❑ Just okay   ❑ Not my thing

....   ❑ Loved it!   ❑ Liked it!   ❑ Just okay   ❑ Not my thing

....   ❑ Loved it!   ❑ Liked it!   ❑ Just okay   ❑ Not my thing

....   ❑ Loved it!   ❑ Liked it!   ❑ Just okay   ❑ Not my thing

TITLE: ....

AUTHOR: ....

INITIALS: RATING:

....   ☐ Loved it!   ☐ Liked it!   ☐ Just okay   ☐ Not my thing

....   ☐ Loved it!   ☐ Liked it!   ☐ Just okay   ☐ Not my thing

....   ☐ Loved it!   ☐ Liked it!   ☐ Just okay   ☐ Not my thing

....   ☐ Loved it!   ☐ Liked it!   ☐ Just okay   ☐ Not my thing

....   ☐ Loved it!   ☐ Liked it!   ☐ Just okay   ☐ Not my thing

....   ☐ Loved it!   ☐ Liked it!   ☐ Just okay   ☐ Not my thing

....   ☐ Loved it!   ☐ Liked it!   ☐ Just okay   ☐ Not my thing

....   ☐ Loved it!   ☐ Liked it!   ☐ Just okay   ☐ Not my thing

....   ☐ Loved it!   ☐ Liked it!   ☐ Just okay   ☐ Not my thing

....   ☐ Loved it!   ☐ Liked it!   ☐ Just okay   ☐ Not my thing

....   ☐ Loved it!   ☐ Liked it!   ☐ Just okay   ☐ Not my thing

....   ☐ Loved it!   ☐ Liked it!   ☐ Just okay   ☐ Not my thing

....   ☐ Loved it!   ☐ Liked it!   ☐ Just okay   ☐ Not my thing

....   ☐ Loved it!   ☐ Liked it!   ☐ Just okay   ☐ Not my thing

....   ☐ Loved it!   ☐ Liked it!   ☐ Just okay   ☐ Not my thing

....   ☐ Loved it!   ☐ Liked it!   ☐ Just okay   ☐ Not my thing

....   ☐ Loved it!   ☐ Liked it!   ☐ Just okay   ☐ Not my thing

....   ☐ Loved it!   ☐ Liked it!   ☐ Just okay   ☐ Not my thing

Check out the books my friends and I have been reading!

TITLE: . . . .

AUTHOR: . . . .

INITIALS: RATING:

. . . .   ❑ Loved it!   ❑ Liked it!   ❑ Just okay   ❑ Not my thing

. . . .   ❑ Loved it!   ❑ Liked it!   ❑ Just okay   ❑ Not my thing

. . . .   ❑ Loved it!   ❑ Liked it!   ❑ Just okay   ❑ Not my thing

. . . .   ❑ Loved it!   ❑ Liked it!   ❑ Just okay   ❑ Not my thing

. . . .   ❑ Loved it!   ❑ Liked it!   ❑ Just okay   ❑ Not my thing

. . . .   ❑ Loved it!   ❑ Liked it!   ❑ Just okay   ❑ Not my thing

. . . .   ❑ Loved it!   ❑ Liked it!   ❑ Just okay   ❑ Not my thing

. . . .   ❑ Loved it!   ❑ Liked it!   ❑ Just okay   ❑ Not my thing

. . . .   ❑ Loved it!   ❑ Liked it!   ❑ Just okay   ❑ Not my thing

. . . .   ❑ Loved it!   ❑ Liked it!   ❑ Just okay   ❑ Not my thing

. . . .   ❑ Loved it!   ❑ Liked it!   ❑ Just okay   ❑ Not my thing

. . . .   ❑ Loved it!   ❑ Liked it!   ❑ Just okay   ❑ Not my thing

. . . .   ❑ Loved it!   ❑ Liked it!   ❑ Just okay   ❑ Not my thing

. . . .   ❑ Loved it!   ❑ Liked it!   ❑ Just okay   ❑ Not my thing

. . . .   ❑ Loved it!   ❑ Liked it!   ❑ Just okay   ❑ Not my thing

. . . .   ❑ Loved it!   ❑ Liked it!   ❑ Just okay   ❑ Not my thing

. . . .   ❑ Loved it!   ❑ Liked it!   ❑ Just okay   ❑ Not my thing

TITLE: ....

AUTHOR: ....

INITIALS: RATING:

....   ❏ Loved it!   ❏ Liked it!   ❏ Just okay   ❏ Not my thing

....   ❏ Loved it!   ❏ Liked it!   ❏ Just okay   ❏ Not my thing

....   ❏ Loved it!   ❏ Liked it!   ❏ Just okay   ❏ Not my thing

....   ❏ Loved it!   ❏ Liked it!   ❏ Just okay   ❏ Not my thing

....   ❏ Loved it!   ❏ Liked it!   ❏ Just okay   ❏ Not my thing

....   ❏ Loved it!   ❏ Liked it!   ❏ Just okay   ❏ Not my thing

....   ❏ Loved it!   ❏ Liked it!   ❏ Just okay   ❏ Not my thing

....   ❏ Loved it!   ❏ Liked it!   ❏ Just okay   ❏ Not my thing

....   ❏ Loved it!   ❏ Liked it!   ❏ Just okay   ❏ Not my thing

....   ❏ Loved it!   ❏ Liked it!   ❏ Just okay   ❏ Not my thing

....   ❏ Loved it!   ❏ Liked it!   ❏ Just okay   ❏ Not my thing

....   ❏ Loved it!   ❏ Liked it!   ❏ Just okay   ❏ Not my thing

....   ❏ Loved it!   ❏ Liked it!   ❏ Just okay   ❏ Not my thing

....   ❏ Loved it!   ❏ Liked it!   ❏ Just okay   ❏ Not my thing

....   ❏ Loved it!   ❏ Liked it!   ❏ Just okay   ❏ Not my thing

....   ❏ Loved it!   ❏ Liked it!   ❏ Just okay   ❏ Not my thing

....   ❏ Loved it!   ❏ Liked it!   ❏ Just okay   ❏ Not my thing

Check out the books my friends and I have been reading!

TITLE: ....

AUTHOR: ....

INITIALS: RATING:

....   ❑ Loved it!   ❑ Liked it!   ❑ Just okay   ❑ Not my thing

....   ❑ Loved it!   ❑ Liked it!   ❑ Just okay   ❑ Not my thing

....   ❑ Loved it!   ❑ Liked it!   ❑ Just okay   ❑ Not my thing

....   ❑ Loved it!   ❑ Liked it!   ❑ Just okay   ❑ Not my thing

....   ❑ Loved it!   ❑ Liked it!   ❑ Just okay   ❑ Not my thing

....   ❑ Loved it!   ❑ Liked it!   ❑ Just okay   ❑ Not my thing

....   ❑ Loved it!   ❑ Liked it!   ❑ Just okay   ❑ Not my thing

....   ❑ Loved it!   ❑ Liked it!   ❑ Just okay   ❑ Not my thing

....   ❑ Loved it!   ❑ Liked it!   ❑ Just okay   ❑ Not my thing

....   ❑ Loved it!   ❑ Liked it!   ❑ Just okay   ❑ Not my thing

....   ❑ Loved it!   ❑ Liked it!   ❑ Just okay   ❑ Not my thing

....   ❑ Loved it!   ❑ Liked it!   ❑ Just okay   ❑ Not my thing

....   ❑ Loved it!   ❑ Liked it!   ❑ Just okay   ❑ Not my thing

....   ❑ Loved it!   ❑ Liked it!   ❑ Just okay   ❑ Not my thing

....   ❑ Loved it!   ❑ Liked it!   ❑ Just okay   ❑ Not my thing

....   ❑ Loved it!   ❑ Liked it!   ❑ Just okay   ❑ Not my thing

....   ❑ Loved it!   ❑ Liked it!   ❑ Just okay   ❑ Not my thing

Books Borrowed
and Lent

Books Borrowed

TITLE: ....

FROM: ....

DATE: ....

TITLE: ....

FROM: ....

DATE: ....

TITLE: ....

FROM: ....

DATE: ....

TITLE: ....

FROM: ....

DATE: ....

TITLE: ....

FROM: ....

DATE: ....

TITLE: ....

FROM: ....

DATE: ....

TITLE: ....

FROM: ....

DATE: ....

TITLE: ....

FROM: ....

DATE: ....

TITLE: ....

FROM: ....

DATE: ....

TITLE: ....

FROM: ....

DATE: ....

Books Borrowed

TITLE: ....

FROM: ....

DATE: ....

TITLE: ....

FROM: ....

DATE: ....

TITLE: ....

FROM: ....

DATE: ....

TITLE: ....

FROM: ....

DATE: ....

TITLE: ....

FROM: ....

DATE: ....

TITLE: ....

FROM: ....

DATE: ....

TITLE: ....

FROM: ....

DATE: ....

TITLE: ....

FROM: ....

DATE: ....

TITLE: ....

FROM: ....

DATE: ....

TITLE: ....

FROM: ....

DATE: ....

Books Borrowed

TITLE: ....

FROM: ....

DATE: ....

TITLE: ....

FROM: ....

DATE: ....

TITLE: ....

FROM: ....

DATE: ....

TITLE: ....

FROM: ....

DATE: ....

TITLE: ....

FROM: ....

DATE: ....

TITLE: ....

FROM: ....

DATE: ....

TITLE: ....

FROM: ....

DATE: ....

TITLE: ....

FROM: ....

DATE: ....

TITLE: ....

FROM: ....

DATE: ....

TITLE: ....

FROM: ....

DATE: ....

Books Borrowed

TITLE: ....
FROM: ....
DATE: ....

TITLE: ....
FROM: ....
DATE: ....

TITLE: ....
FROM: ....
DATE: ....

TITLE: ....
FROM: ....
DATE: ....

TITLE: ....
FROM: ....
DATE: ....

TITLE: ....
FROM: ....
DATE: ....

TITLE: ....
FROM: ....
DATE: ....

TITLE: ....
FROM: ....
DATE: ....

TITLE: ....
FROM: ....
DATE: ....

TITLE: ....
FROM: ....
DATE: ....

Books Lent

TITLE: New Moon

FROM: Me to Stephanie

DATE: Long agooooo

TITLE:

FROM:

DATE:

TITLE:

FROM:

DATE:

TITLE:

FROM:

DATE:

TITLE:

FROM:

DATE:

TITLE: ....

FROM: ....

DATE: ....

TITLE: ....

FROM: ....

DATE: ....

TITLE: ....

FROM: ....

DATE: ....

TITLE: ....

FROM: ....

DATE: ....

TITLE: ....

FROM: ....

DATE: ....

Books Lent

TITLE: ....

FROM: ....

DATE: ....

TITLE: ....

FROM: ....

DATE: ....

TITLE: ....

FROM: ....

DATE: ....

TITLE: ....

FROM: ....

DATE: ....

TITLE: ....

FROM: ....

DATE: ....

TITLE: ....
FROM: ....
DATE: ....

TITLE: ....
FROM: ....
DATE: ....

TITLE: ....
FROM: ....
DATE: ....

TITLE: ....
FROM: ....
DATE: ....

TITLE: ....
FROM: ....
DATE: ....

Books Lent

TITLE: ....

FROM: ....

DATE: ....

TITLE: ....

FROM: ....

DATE: ....

TITLE: ....

FROM: ....

DATE: ....

TITLE: ....

FROM: ....

DATE: ....

TITLE: ....

FROM: ....

DATE: ....

TITLE: ....
FROM: ....
DATE: ....

TITLE: ....
FROM: ....
DATE: ....

TITLE: ....
FROM: ....
DATE: ....

TITLE: ....
FROM: ....
DATE: ....

TITLE: ....
FROM: ....
DATE: ....

Books Lent

TITLE: ....
FROM: ....
DATE: ....

TITLE: ....
FROM: ....
DATE: ....

TITLE: ....
FROM: ....
DATE: ....

TITLE: ....
FROM: ....
DATE: ....

TITLE: ....
FROM: ....
DATE: ....

TITLE: ....

FROM: ....

DATE: ....

TITLE: ....

FROM: ....

DATE: ....

TITLE: ....

FROM: ....

DATE: ....

TITLE: ....

FROM: ....

DATE: ....

TITLE: ....

FROM: ....

DATE: ....

About the Author

Nancy Pearl's first job out of library school was as a children's librarian, and since then she has worked as a librarian and bookseller in Detroit, Tulsa, and Seattle. In 1998, she developed the program "If All of Seattle Read the Same Book," which has been replicated in communities around the globe. The former Executive Director of the Washington Center for the Book, Pearl celebrates the written word by speaking at bookstores, community groups, and libraries across the country. She is a regular commentator about books on National Public Radio's *Morning Edition* and NPR affiliate stations KUOW in Seattle and KWGS in Tulsa, and is the model for the Librarian Action Figure. She is the author of *Book Lust*, *More Book Lust*, and *Book Crush*.

In 2004, Pearl became the fiftieth winner of the Women's National Book Association Award for her extraordinary contribution to the world of books. In the moment when Pearls find herself without a book, she is an avid bicyclist and happy grandmother of two. She lives in Seattle with her husband, Joe.